A Word to Parents –

This book grew out of a desire to provide a companion study journal for children for use alongside the Growing Through Prayer adult study journal.

Love God Greatly is dedicated to making God's Word available to our beautiful community of women… and now, women have the opportunity to share God's Word with children through this study uniquely crafted for young hearts.

The Intro to Growing Through Prayer for Kids (pg. 4) may assist you in preparing your child for the weeks ahead. We are excited about this new resource that offers God's Word to the next generation of believers, and we praise God that you are a part of this adventure!

Table of contents

Intro to Prayer

Hi! We're glad you're here!

This study is about PRAYER.

God talks a lot about prayer in the Bible!

Since He encourages us to pray ALL the time, it must be important, don't you think?

Let's talk about what makes it so important!

Prayer is a gift

When we pray we are TALKING to God.

We are able to speak with him WHENEVER we want! Sometimes we don't want to tell people what we are THINKING because we are embarrassed.

We believe others wouldn't UNDERSTAND or that they would think we are SILLY. But through the gift of prayer, we get to tell God ANYTHING we want ANY TIME we want! And He ALWAYS listens and NEVER thinks we are silly…

Prayer allows God to help us

Many times we need HELP but we are too proud to ASK.

We may need help with our FRIENDSHIPS, our SIBLINGS, our PARENTS, our SCHOOL WORK, or even with our own THOUGHTS or ACTIONS.

God wants to help us get through every day of our life and we bring JOY to His heart when we come to Him and ask for His help.

Who is God?

God is the maker of heaven and earth. He made ALL things and He made US. He knows what we NEED before we do. What makes God different than anyone else is that God is HOLY, which means He cannot sin. God is RIGHTEOUS, which means He does everything right. God is PURE, which means He is spotless and clean and there is nothing unclean about Him.

Intro to Prayer

Who are we?

We are God's creation. He made us to have relationship with himself. Sin caused man to be separated from a HOLY God.

God loved us so MUCH He made a way for us to be in relationship with Him. He sent His son JESUS to die for our sins and made a way·for us to be in God's presence.

Because of JESUS, we can have a RELATIONSHIP with God, we can PRAY to GOD and we can be with GOD forever!

Growing through prayer

JESUS set an EXAMPLE for us in the way He prayed to God, His father.

He made prayer a part of His DAILY life and we are encouraged to do the same.

Prayer is important because:
- It refocuses our eyes on Jesus
- It gives us strength
- It draws us close to God
- It brings comfort
- It produces peace
- It explodes our love for God
- It is a hiding place during times of sadness and pain
- It is a place of healing when we hurt
- It is a time to ask for help
- It is a time of praise and worship to God

Through this study, we will learn HOW to pray, WHAT to pray for, and if God really does HEAR our prayers!

Let's get started!!!!!

Goals

We believe it's important to write out goals for each session. Take some time now and write three goals you would like to focus on this session as we begin to rise each day and dig into God's Word. Make sure and refer back to these goals throughout the next eight weeks to help you stay focused. YOU CAN DO IT!!!

My goals for this session are:

1.

2.

3.

Signature: _____

Date: _____

Reading Plan

		Read	Write
WEEK 1	Monday	Acts 2:41-47	Acts 2:42
	Tuesday	Hebrews 4:15-16	Hebrews 4:16
	Wednesday	Jeremiah 10:6-7	Jeremiah 10:6-7
	Thursday	Psalm 145:1-7	Psalm 145:1-2
	Friday	Romans 15:30; Colossians 1:9	Colossians 1:9
	Review		
WEEK 2	Monday	1 Timothy 2:8	1 Timothy 2:8
	Tuesday	Mark 1:35; Matthew 14:23	Mark 1:35
	Wednesday	Acts 9:40	Acts 9:40
	Thursday	Ephesians 3:14-16	Ephesians 3:14-16
	Friday	John 15:1-5	John 15:5
	Review		
WEEK 3	Monday	Psalm 145:1-13	Psalm 145:1-3
	Tuesday	Isaiah 6:1-6	Isaiah 6:5
	Wednesday	Philippians 4:5–7	Philippians 4:6
	Thursday	Hebrews 13:15	Hebrews 13:15
	Friday	Psalm 140	Psalm 140:9-11
	Review		
WEEK 4	Monday	Psalm 62	Psalm 62:8
	Tuesday	Psalm 37:7-8	Psalm 37:7-8
	Wednesday	Luke 18:1-7	Luke 18:1,7
	Thursday	Mark 11:23-24	Mark 11:24
	Friday	Colossians 4:2; 1 Thessalonians 5:17	1 Thessalonians 5:17
	Review		
WEEK 5	Monday	Ephesians 1:15-18	Ephesians 1:17
	Tuesday	Matthew 26:40-41	Matthew 26:41
	Wednesday	Colossians 1:3-12	Colossians 1:3-4
	Thursday	1 Timothy 2:1-3	1 Timothy 2:1-2
	Friday	Luke 6:27-28	Luke 6:27-28
	Review		
WEEK 6	Monday	Romans 5:1-2	Romans 5:2
	Tuesday	1 John 5:13-15	1 John 5:14
	Wednesday	Isaiah 41:10; Psalm 34:18	Psalm 34:18
	Thursday	Matthew 7:7-11	Matthew 7:11
	Friday	Romans 8:26-27	Romans 8:27
	Review		
WEEK 7	Monday	2 Corinthians 12:7-10	2 Corinthians 12:8-9
	Tuesday	1 Samuel 1:1-20	1 Samuel 1:20
	Wednesday	Psalm 37:7; Lamentations 3:25	Psalm 37:7
	Thursday	1 Kings 18:20-39	1 Kings 18:38-39
	Friday	John 1:16; Ephesians 3:20-21	John 1:16; Ephesians 3:20
	Review		
WEEK 8	Monday	Psalm 5:3; Proverbs 8:17	Psalm 5:3
	Tuesday	Psalm 63:5-8	Psalm 63:5-6
	Wednesday	Psalm 100	Psalm 100:4-5
	Thursday	Psalm 18:1-6	Psalm 18:6
	Friday	Psalm 51	Psalm 51:2-4
	Review		

Week 1

Prayer focus for this week: Spend time praying for your family members.

	Praying	Praise
Monday		
Tuesday		
Wednesday		
Thursday		
Friday		

LET US THEN WITH CONFIDENCE DRAW NEAR TO THE THRONE OF GRACE, THAT WE MAY RECEIVE MERCY AND FIND GRACE TO HELP IN TIME OF NEED.

Hebrews 4:16

Week 1

SCRIPTURE FOR THIS WEEK

Acts 2:41-47 ESV

[41] So those who received his word were baptized, and there were added that day about three thousand souls. [42] And they devoted themselves to the apostles' teaching and the fellowship, to the breaking of bread and the prayers. [43] And awe came upon every soul, and many wonders and signs were being done through the apostles. [44] And all who believed were together and had all things in common. [45] And they were selling their possessions and belongings and distributing the proceeds to all, as any had need. [46] And day by day, attending the temple together and breaking bread in their homes, they received their food with glad and generous hearts, [47] praising God and having favor with all the people. And the Lord added to their number day by day those who were being saved.

Hebrews 4:15-16 ESV

[15] For we do not have a high priest who is unable to sympathize with our weaknesses, but one who in every respect has been tempted as we are, yet without sin. [16] Let us then with confidence draw near to the throne of grace, that we may receive mercy and find grace to help in time of need.

Jeremiah 10:6-7 ESV

[6] There is none like you, O Lord; you are great, and your name is great in might. [7] Who would not fear you, O King of the nations? For this is your due; for among all the wise ones of the nations and in all their kingdoms there is none like you.

Week 1

SCRIPTURE FOR THIS WEEK

Psalm 145:1-7 ESV

I will extol you, my God and King, and bless your name forever and ever. [2] Every day I will bless you and praise your name forever and ever. [3] Great is the Lord, and greatly to be praised, and his greatness is unsearchable.

[4] One generation shall commend your works to another, and shall declare your mighty acts. [5] On the glorious splendor of your majesty, and on your wondrous works, I will meditate. [6] They shall speak of the might of your awesome deeds, and I will declare your greatness. [7] They shall pour forth the fame of your abundant goodness and shall sing aloud of your righteousness.

Romans 15:30 ESV

[30] I appeal to you, brothers, by our Lord Jesus Christ and by the love of the Spirit, to strive together with me in your prayers to God on my behalf.

Colossians 1:9 ESV

[9] And so, from the day we heard, we have not ceased to pray for you, asking that you may be filled with the knowledge of his will in all spiritual wisdom and understanding,

Monday

READ: Acts 2:41-47   WRITE: Acts 2:42

1. Write out today's **SCRIPTURE** passage.

_____

_____

_____

_____

_____

_____

_____

_____

_____

_____

2. On the blank page to the right, **DRAW** or **WRITE** what this passage means to you.

3. My **PRAYER** for today:

_____

_____

_____

_____

LoveGodGreatly.com

Monday

Tuesday

READ: Hebrews 4:15-16   WRITE: Hebrews 4:16

1. Write out today's **SCRIPTURE** passage.

_____

_____

_____

_____

_____

_____

_____

_____

_____

2. On the blank page to the right, **DRAW** or **WRITE** what this passage means to you.

3. My **PRAYER** for today:

_____

_____

_____

_____

Tuesday

Wednesday

Jeremiah 10:6-7

WRITE: Jeremiah 10:6-7

1. Write out today's **SCRIPTURE** passage.

_____

_____

_____

_____

_____

_____

_____

_____

_____

_____

2. On the blank page to the right, **DRAW** or **WRITE** what this passage means to you.

3. My **PRAYER** for today:

_____

_____

_____

_____

_____

LoveGodGreatly.com

Wednesday

Thursday

READ: Psalm 145:1-7   WRITE: Psalm 145:1-2

1. Write out today's **SCRIPTURE** passage.

_____

_____

_____

_____

_____

_____

_____

_____

_____

2. On the blank page to the right, **DRAW** or **WRITE** what this passage means to you.

3. My **PRAYER** for today:

_____

_____

_____

_____

_____

LoveGodGreatly.com

Thursday

Friday

READ: Romans 15:30; Colossians 1:9   **WRITE**: Colossians 1:9

1. Write out today's **SCRIPTURE** passage.

_____

_____

_____

_____

_____

_____

_____

_____

2. On the blank page to the right, **DRAW** or **WRITE** what this passage means to you.

3. My **PRAYER** for today:

_____

_____

_____

_____

Friday

This week I learned...

WEEK 1

Use the space below to draw a picture or write about what you learned this week from your time in God's Word.

Week 2

Prayer focus for this week: Spend time praying for your country.

	Praying	Praise
Monday		
Tuesday		
Wednesday		
Thursday		
Friday		

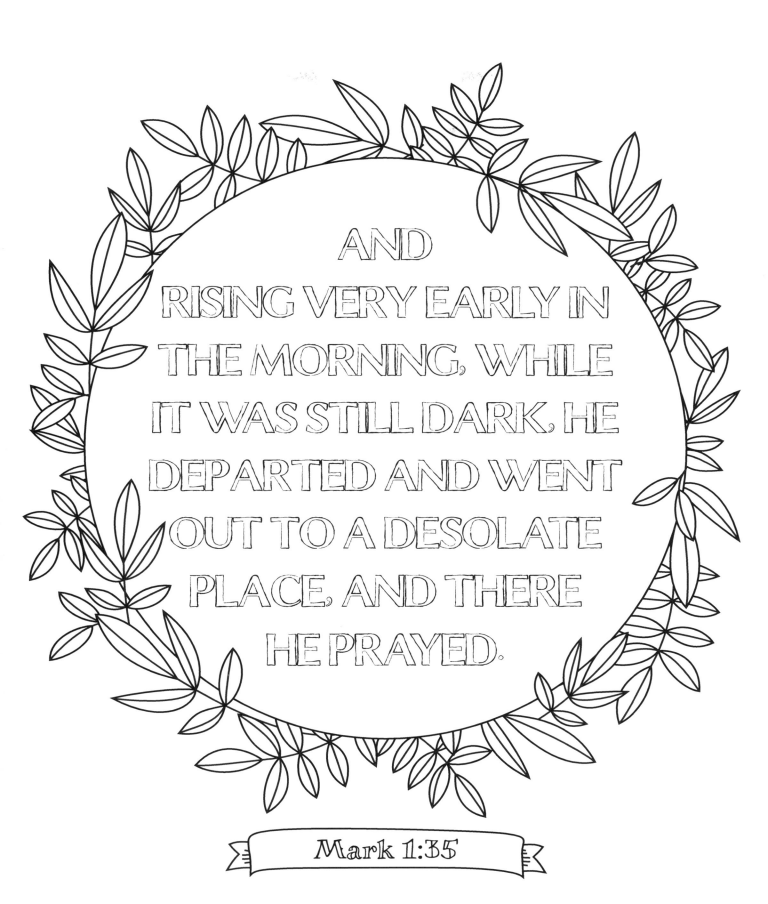

AND
RISING VERY EARLY IN
THE MORNING, WHILE
IT WAS STILL DARK, HE
DEPARTED AND WENT
OUT TO A DESOLATE
PLACE, AND THERE
HE PRAYED.

Mark 1:35

Week 2

SCRIPTURE FOR THIS WEEK

1 Timothy 2:8 ESV

8 I desire then that in every place the men should pray, lifting holy hands without anger or quarreling;

Mark 1:35 ESV

35 And rising very early in the morning, while it was still dark, he departed and went out to a desolate place, and there he prayed.

Matthew 14:23 ESV

23 And after he had dismissed the crowds, he went up on the mountain by himself to pray. When evening came, he was there alone,

Acts 9:40 ESV

40 But Peter put them all outside, and knelt down and prayed; and turning to the body he said, "Tabitha, arise." And she opened her eyes, and when she saw Peter she sat up.

Ephesians 3:14-16 ESV

14 For this reason I bow my knees before the Father, 15 from whom every family in heaven and on earth is named, 16 that according to the riches of his glory he may grant you to be strengthened with power through his Spirit in your inner being,

SCRIPTURE FOR THIS WEEK

John 15:1-5 ESV

"I am the true vine, and my Father is the vinedresser. [2] Every branch in me that does not bear fruit he takes away, and every branch that does bear fruit he prunes, that it may bear more fruit. [3] Already you are clean because of the word that I have spoken to you. [4] Abide in me, and I in you. As the branch cannot bear fruit by itself, unless it abides in the vine, neither can you, unless you abide in me. [5] I am the vine; you are the branches. Whoever abides in me and I in him, he it is that bears much fruit, for apart from me you can do nothing.

Monday

READ: 1 Timothy 2:8   **WRITE:** 1 Timothy 2:8

1. Write out today's **SCRIPTURE** passage.

_____

_____

_____

_____

_____

_____

_____

_____

_____

2. On the blank page to the right, **DRAW** or **WRITE** what this passage means to you.

3. My **PRAYER** for today:

_____

_____

_____

_____

_____

Monday

Tuesday

READ: Mark 1:35; Matthew 14:23   WRITE: Mark 1:35

1. Write out today's **SCRIPTURE** passage.

_____

_____

_____

_____

_____

_____

_____

_____

_____

2. On the blank page to the right, **DRAW** or **WRITE** what this passage means to you.

3. My **PRAYER** for today:

_____

_____

_____

_____

Tuesday

READ: Acts 9:40   WRITE: Acts 9:40

1. Write out today's **SCRIPTURE** passage.

_____

_____

_____

_____

_____

_____

_____

_____

2. On the blank page to the right, **DRAW** or **WRITE** what this passage means to you.

3. My **PRAYER** for today:

_____

_____

_____

_____

Wednesday

Thursday

READ: Ephesians 3:14-16   WRITE: Ephesians 3:14-16

1. Write out today's SCRIPTURE passage.

_____

_____

_____

_____

_____

_____

_____

_____

_____

_____

2. On the blank page to the right, DRAW or WRITE what this passage means to you.

3. My PRAYER for today:

_____

_____

_____

_____

_____

Thursday

Friday

READ: John 15:1-5   WRITE: John 15:5

1. Write out today's SCRIPTURE passage.

_____

_____

_____

_____

_____

_____

_____

_____

_____

2. On the blank page to the right, DRAW or WRITE what this passage means to you.

3. My PRAYER for today:

_____

_____

_____

_____

_____

Friday

This week I learned...

WEEK 2

Use the space below to draw a picture or write about what you learned this week from your time in God's Word.

Prayer focus for this week: Spend time praying for your friends.

	Praying	Praise
Monday		
Tuesday		
Wednesday		
Thursday		
Friday		

THROUGH HIM THEN LET US CONTINUALLY OFFER UP A SACRIFICE OF PRAISE TO GOD, THAT IS, THE FRUIT OF LIPS THAT ACKNOWLEDGE HIS NAME.

Hebrews 13:15

Week 3

SCRIPTURE FOR THIS WEEK

Psalm 145:1-13 ESV

I will extol you, my God and King, and bless your name forever and ever. [2] Every day I will bless you and praise your name forever and ever. [3] Great is the Lord, and greatly to be praised, and his greatness is unsearchable.

[4] One generation shall commend your works to another, and shall declare your mighty acts. [5] On the glorious splendor of your majesty, and on your wondrous works, I will meditate. [6] They shall speak of the might of your awesome deeds, and I will declare your greatness. [7] They shall pour forth the fame of your abundant goodness and shall sing aloud of your righteousness.

[8] The Lord is gracious and merciful, slow to anger and abounding in steadfast love. [9] The Lord is good to all, and his mercy is over all that he has made.

[10] All your works shall give thanks to you, O Lord, and all your saints shall bless you! [11] They shall speak of the glory of your kingdom and tell of your power, [12] to make known to the children of man your mighty deeds, and the glorious splendor of your kingdom. [13] Your kingdom is an everlasting kingdom, and your dominion endures throughout all generations. [The Lord is faithful in all his words and kind in all his works.]

Isaiah 6:1-6 ESV

In the year that King Uzziah died I saw the Lord sitting upon a throne, high and lifted up; and the train of his robe filled the temple. [2] Above him stood the seraphim. Each had six wings: with two he covered his face, and with two he covered his feet, and with two he flew. [3] And one called to another and said: "Holy, holy, holy is the Lord of hosts; the whole earth is full of his glory!"

[4] And the foundations of the thresholds shook at the voice of him who called, and the house was filled with smoke. [5] And I said: "Woe is me! For I am lost; for I am a man of unclean lips, and I dwell in the midst of a people of unclean lips; for my eyes have seen the King, the Lord of hosts!" [6] Then one of the seraphim flew to me, having in his hand a burning coal that he had taken with tongs from the altar.

Week 3

SCRIPTURE FOR THIS WEEK

Philippians 4:5-7 ESV

[5] Let your reasonableness be known to everyone. The Lord is at hand; [6] do not be anxious about anything, but in everything by prayer and supplication with thanksgiving let your requests be made known to God. [7] And the peace of God, which surpasses all understanding, will guard your hearts and your minds in Christ Jesus.

Hebrews 13:15 ESV

[15] Through him then let us continually offer up a sacrifice of praise to God, that is, the fruit of lips that acknowledge his name.

Psalm 140 ESV

Deliver me, O Lord, from evil men; preserve me from violent men, [2] who plan evil things in their heart and stir up wars continually. [3] They make their tongue sharp as a serpent's, and under their lips is the venom of asps.

[4] Guard me, O Lord, from the hands of the wicked; preserve me from violent men, who have planned to trip up my feet. [5] The arrogant have hidden a trap for me, and with cords they have spread a net; beside the way they have set snares for me.

[6] I say to the Lord, You are my God; give ear to the voice of my pleas for mercy, O Lord! [7] O Lord, my Lord, the strength of my salvation, you have covered my head in the day of battle. [8] Grant not, O Lord, the desires of the wicked; do not further their[b] evil plot, or they will be exalted!

[9] As for the head of those who surround me, let the mischief of their lips overwhelm them! [10] Let burning coals fall upon them! Let them be cast into fire, into miry pits, no more to rise! [11] Let not the slanderer be established in the land; let evil hunt down the violent man speedily!

[12] I know that the Lord will maintain the cause of the afflicted, and will execute justice for the needy. [13] Surely the righteous shall give thanks to your name; the upright shall dwell in your presence.

Monday

READ: Psalm 145:1-13   **WRITE:** Psalm 145:1-3

1. Write out today's **SCRIPTURE** passage.

_____

_____

_____

_____

_____

_____

_____

_____

2. On the blank page to the right, **DRAW** or **WRITE** what this passage means to you.

3. My **PRAYER** for today:

_____

_____

_____

_____

Monday

Tuesday

1. Write out today's **SCRIPTURE** passage.

_____

_____

_____

_____

_____

_____

_____

_____

_____

_____

2. On the blank page to the right, **DRAW** or **WRITE** what this passage means to you.

3. My **PRAYER** for today:

_____

_____

_____

_____

_____

Tuesday

Wednesday

READ: Philippians 4:5-7   **WRITE:** Philippians 4:6

1. Write out today's **SCRIPTURE** passage.

_____

_____

_____

_____

_____

_____

_____

_____

_____

2. On the blank page to the right, **DRAW** or **WRITE** what this passage means to you.

3. My **PRAYER** for today:

_____

_____

_____

_____

_____

Wednesday

Thursday

READ: Hebrews 13:15   WRITE: Hebrews 13:15

1. Write out today's **SCRIPTURE** passage.

_____

_____

_____

_____

_____

_____

_____

_____

_____

2. On the blank page to the right, **DRAW** or **WRITE** what this passage means to you.

3. My **PRAYER** for today:

_____

_____

_____

_____

_____

Thursday

Friday

READ: Psalm 140   WRITE: Psalm 140:9-11

1. Write out today's **SCRIPTURE** passage.

_____

_____

_____

_____

_____

_____

_____

_____

_____

2. On the blank page to the right, **DRAW** or **WRITE** what this passage means to you.

3. My **PRAYER** for today:

_____

_____

_____

_____

_____

Friday

This week I learned...

WEEK 3

Use the space below to draw a picture or write about what you learned this week from your time in God's Word.

Prayer focus for this week: Spend time praying for your church.

	Praying	Praise
Monday		
Tuesday		
Wednesday		
Thursday		
Friday		

AND HE TOLD THEM A PARABLE TO THE EFFECT THAT THEY OUGHT ALWAYS TO PRAY AND NOT LOSE HEART.

Luke 18:1

SCRIPTURE FOR THIS WEEK

Psalm 62 ESV

For God alone my soul waits in silence; from him comes my salvation. ² He alone is my rock and my salvation, my fortress; I shall not be greatly shaken.

³ How long will all of you attack a man to batter him, like a leaning wall, a tottering fence? ⁴ They only plan to thrust him down from his high position. They take pleasure in falsehood. They bless with their mouths, but inwardly they curse.

⁵ For God alone, O my soul, wait in silence, for my hope is from him. ⁶ He only is my rock and my salvation, my fortress; I shall not be shaken. ⁷ On God rests my salvation and my glory; my mighty rock, my refuge is God.

⁸ Trust in him at all times, O people; pour out your heart before him; God is a refuge for us.

⁹ Those of low estate are but a breath; those of high estate are a delusion; in the balances they go up; they are together lighter than a breath. ¹⁰ Put no trust in extortion; set no vain hopes on robbery; if riches increase, set not your heart on them.

¹¹ Once God has spoken; twice have I heard this: that power belongs to God, ¹² and that to you, O Lord, belongs steadfast love. For you will render to a man according to his work.

Psalm 37:7-8 ESV

⁷ Be still before the Lord and wait patiently for him; fret not yourself over the one who prospers in his way, over the man who carries out evil devices!

⁸ Refrain from anger, and forsake wrath! Fret not yourself; it tends only to evil.

Luke 18:1-7 ESV

And he told them a parable to the effect that they ought always to pray and not lose heart. ² He said, "In a certain city there was a judge who neither feared God nor respected man. ³ And there was a widow in that city who kept coming to him and saying, 'Give me justice against my adversary.'

SCRIPTURE FOR THIS WEEK

[4] For a while he refused, but afterward he said to himself, 'Though I neither fear God nor respect man, [5] yet because this widow keeps bothering me, I will give her justice, so that she will not beat me down by her continual coming.'" [6] And the Lord said, "Hear what the unrighteous judge says. [7] And will not God give justice to his elect, who cry to him day and night? Will he delay long over them?

Mark 11:23-24 ESV

[23] Truly, I say to you, whoever says to this mountain, 'Be taken up and thrown into the sea,' and does not doubt in his heart, but believes that what he says will come to pass, it will be done for him. [24] Therefore I tell you, whatever you ask in prayer, believe that you have received it, and it will be yours.

Colossians 4:2 ESV

[2] Continue steadfastly in prayer, being watchful in it with thanksgiving.

1 Thessalonians 5:17 ESV

[17] pray without ceasing,

Monday

READ: Psalm 62   **WRITE**: Psalm 62:8

1. Write out today's **SCRIPTURE** passage.

_____

_____

_____

_____

_____

_____

_____

_____

_____

2. On the blank page to the right, **DRAW** or **WRITE** what this passage means to you.

3. My **PRAYER** for today:

_____

_____

_____

_____

_____

Monday

Tuesday

READ: Psalm 37:7-8   WRITE: Psalm 37:7-8

1. Write out today's **SCRIPTURE** passage.

_____

_____

_____

_____

_____

_____

_____

_____

2. On the blank page to the right, **DRAW** or **WRITE** what this passage means to you.

3. My **PRAYER** for today:

_____

_____

_____

_____

Tuesday

Wednesday

READ: Luke 18:1-7   WRITE: Luke 18:1, 7

1. Write out today's SCRIPTURE passage.

_____

_____

_____

_____

_____

_____

_____

_____

_____

_____

2. On the blank page to the right, DRAW or WRITE what this passage means to you.

3. My PRAYER for today:

_____

_____

_____

_____

_____

Wednesday

Thursday

READ: Mark 11:23-24   WRITE: Mark 11:24

1. Write out today's SCRIPTURE passage.

_____

_____

_____

_____

_____

_____

_____

_____

_____

2. On the blank page to the right, DRAW or WRITE what this passage means to you.

3. My PRAYER for today:

_____

_____

_____

_____

LoveGodGreatly.com

Thursday

Friday

READ: Colossians 4:2; 1 Thessalonians 5:17   WRITE: 1 Thessalonians 5:17

1. Write out today's **SCRIPTURE** passage.

_____

_____

_____

_____

_____

_____

_____

_____

_____

2. On the blank page to the right, **DRAW** or **WRITE** what this passage means to you.

3. My **PRAYER** for today:

_____

_____

_____

_____

LoveGodGreatly.com

Friday

This week I learned...

WEEK 4

Use the space below to draw a picture or write about what you learned this week from your time in God's Word.

Prayer focus for this week: Spend time praying for missionaries.

	Praying	Praise
Monday		
Tuesday		
Wednesday		
Thursday		
Friday		

BUT I SAY TO YOU WHO HEAR, LOVE YOUR ENEMIES, DO GOOD TO THOSE WHO HATE YOU, BLESS THOSE WHO CURSE YOU, PRAY FOR THOSE WHO ABUSE YOU.

Luke 6:27-28

Week 5

SCRIPTURE FOR THIS WEEK

Ephesians 1:15-18 ESV

¹⁵ For this reason, because I have heard of your faith in the Lord Jesus and your love toward all the saints, ¹⁶ I do not cease to give thanks for you, remembering you in my prayers, ¹⁷ that the God of our Lord Jesus Christ, the Father of glory, may give you the Spirit of wisdom and of revelation in the knowledge of him, ¹⁸ having the eyes of your hearts enlightened, that you may know what is the hope to which he has called you, what are the riches of his glorious inheritance in the saints,

Matthew 26:40-41 ESV

⁴⁰ And he came to the disciples and found them sleeping. And he said to Peter, "So, could you not watch with me one hour? ⁴¹ Watch and pray that you may not enter into temptation. The spirit indeed is willing, but the flesh is weak."

Colossians 1:3-12 ESV

³ We always thank God, the Father of our Lord Jesus Christ, when we pray for you, ⁴ since we heard of your faith in Christ Jesus and of the love that you have for all the saints, ⁵ because of the hope laid up for you in heaven. Of this you have heard before in the word of the truth, the gospel, ⁶ which has come to you, as indeed in the whole world it is bearing fruit and increasing—as it also does among you, since the day you heard it and understood the grace of God in truth, ⁷ just as you learned it from Epaphras our beloved fellow servant. He is a faithful minister of Christ on your behalf ⁸ and has made known to us your love in the Spirit.

⁹ And so, from the day we heard, we have not ceased to pray for you, asking that you may be filled with the knowledge of his will in all spiritual wisdom and understanding, ¹⁰ so as to walk in a manner worthy of the Lord, fully pleasing to him, bearing fruit in every good work and increasing in the knowledge of God. ¹¹ May you be strengthened with all power, according to

his glorious might, for all endurance and patience with joy, ¹² giving thanks to the Father, who has qualified you[e] to share in the inheritance of the saints in light.

Week 5

SCRIPTURE FOR THIS WEEK

1 Timothy 2:1-3 ESV

First of all, then, I urge that supplications, prayers, intercessions, and thanksgivings be made for all people, [2] for kings and all who are in high positions, that we may lead a peaceful and quiet life, godly and dignified in every way. [3] This is good, and it is pleasing in the sight of God our Savior,

Luke 6:27-28 ESV

[27] "But I say to you who hear, Love your enemies, do good to those who hate you, [28] bless those who curse you, pray for those who abuse you.

Monday

READ: Ephesians 1:15-18   WRITE: Ephesians 1:17

1. Write out today's **SCRIPTURE** passage.

_____

_____

_____

_____

_____

_____

_____

_____

_____

2. On the blank page to the right, **DRAW** or **WRITE** what this passage means to you.

3. My **PRAYER** for today:

_____

_____

_____

_____

_____

Monday

Tuesday

READ: Matthew 26:40-41   **WRITE**: Matthew 26:41

1. Write out today's **SCRIPTURE** passage.

_____

_____

_____

_____

_____

_____

_____

_____

_____

2. On the blank page to the right, **DRAW** or **WRITE** what this passage means to you.

3. My **PRAYER** for today:

_____

_____

_____

_____

_____

Tuesday

Wednesday

READ: Colossians 1:3-12   **WRITE**: Colossians 1:3-4

1. Write out today's **SCRIPTURE** passage.

_____

_____

_____

_____

_____

_____

_____

_____

_____

_____

2. On the blank page to the right, **DRAW** or **WRITE** what this passage means to you.

3. My **PRAYER** for today:

_____

_____

_____

_____

_____

Wednesday

Thursday

READ: 1 Timothy 2:1-3   **WRITE:** 1 Timothy 2:1-2

1. Write out today's **SCRIPTURE** passage.

_____

_____

_____

_____

_____

_____

_____

_____

_____

2. On the blank page to the right, **DRAW** or **WRITE** what this passage means to you.

3. My **PRAYER** for today:

_____

_____

_____

_____

_____

LoveGodGreatly.com

Thursday

Friday

READ: Luke 6:27-28   WRITE: Luke 6:27-28

1. Write out today's **SCRIPTURE** passage.

_____

_____

_____

_____

_____

_____

_____

_____

_____

_____

2. On the blank page to the right, **DRAW** or **WRITE** what this passage means to you.

3. My **PRAYER** for today:

_____

_____

_____

_____

_____

LoveGodGreatly.com

Friday

This week I learned...

WEEK 5

Use the space below to draw a picture or write about what you learned this week from your time in God's Word.

Prayer focus for this week: Spend time praying for you.

	Praying	Praise
Monday		
Tuesday		
Wednesday		
Thursday		
Friday		

AND THIS IS THE CONFIDENCE THAT WE HAVE TOWARD HIM, THAT IF WE ASK ANYTHING ACCORDING TO HIS WILL HE HEARS US.

1 John 5:14

Week 6

SCRIPTURE FOR THIS WEEK

Romans 5:1-2 ESV

Therefore, since we have been justified by faith, we have peace with God through our Lord Jesus Christ. ² Through him we have also obtained access by faith into this grace in which we stand, and we rejoice in hope of the glory of God.

1 John 5:13-15 ESV

¹³ I write these things to you who believe in the name of the Son of God that you may know that you have eternal life. ¹⁴ And this is the confidence that we have toward him, that if we ask anything according to his will he hears us. ¹⁵ And if we know that he hears us in whatever we ask, we know that we have the requests that we have asked of him.

Isaiah. 41:10 ESV

¹⁰ fear not, for I am with you; be not dismayed, for I am your God; I will strengthen you, I will help you, I will uphold you with my righteous right hand.

Psalm 34:18 ESV

¹⁸ The Lord is near to the brokenhearted and saves the crushed in spirit.

Matthew 7:7-11 ESV

⁷ "Ask, and it will be given to you; seek, and you will find; knock, and it will be opened to you. ⁸ For everyone who asks receives, and the one who seeks finds, and to the one who knocks it will be opened. ⁹ Or which one of you, if his son asks him for bread, will give him a stone? ¹⁰ Or if he asks for a fish, will give him a serpent? ¹¹ If you then, who are evil, know how to give good gifts to your children, how much more will your Father who is in heaven give good things to those who ask him!

Week 6

SCRIPTURE FOR THIS WEEK

Romans 8:26-27 ESV

[26] Likewise the Spirit helps us in our weakness. For we do not know what to pray for as we ought, but the Spirit himself intercedes for us with groanings too deep for words. [27] And he who searches hearts knows what is the mind of the Spirit, because the Spirit intercedes for the saints according to the will of God.

Monday

READ: Romans 5:1-2   **WRITE**: Romans 5:2

1. Write out today's **SCRIPTURE** passage.

_____

_____

_____

_____

_____

_____

_____

_____

_____

_____

2. On the blank page to the right, **DRAW** or **WRITE** what this passage means to you.

3. My **PRAYER** for today:

_____

_____

_____

_____

_____

LoveGodGreatly.com

Monday

Tuesday

READ: 1 John 5:13-15   **WRITE**: 1 John 5:14

1. Write out today's **SCRIPTURE** passage.

_____

_____

_____

_____

_____

_____

_____

_____

_____

_____

2. On the blank page to the right, **DRAW** or **WRITE** what this passage means to you.

3. My **PRAYER** for today:

_____

_____

_____

_____

_____

Tuesday

Wednesday

READ: Isaiah. 41:10; Psalm 34:18   WRITE: Psalm 34:18

1. Write out today's **SCRIPTURE** passage.

_____

_____

_____

_____

_____

_____

_____

_____

_____

2. On the blank page to the right, **DRAW** or **WRITE** what this passage means to you.

3. My **PRAYER** for today:

_____

_____

_____

_____

LoveGodGreatly.com

Wednesday

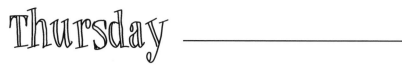

Thursday

READ: Matthew 7:7-11   **WRITE:** Matthew 7:11

1. Write out today's **SCRIPTURE** passage.

_____

_____

_____

_____

_____

_____

_____

_____

_____

_____

2. On the blank page to the right, **DRAW** or **WRITE** what this passage means to you.

3. My **PRAYER** for today:

_____

_____

_____

_____

_____

Thursday

Friday

READ: Romans 8:26-27   WRITE: Romans 8:27

1. Write out today's **SCRIPTURE** passage.

_____

_____

_____

_____

_____

_____

_____

_____

_____

_____

2. On the blank page to the right, **DRAW** or **WRITE** what this passage means to you.

3. My **PRAYER** for today:

_____

_____

_____

_____

LoveGodGreatly.com

Friday

This week I learned...

WEEK 6

Use the space below to draw a picture or write about what you learned this week from your time in God's Word.

LoveGodGreatly.com

Week 7

Prayer focus for this week: Spend time this week turning your fears into prayers.

	Praying	Praise
Monday		
Tuesday		
Wednesday		
Thursday		
Friday		

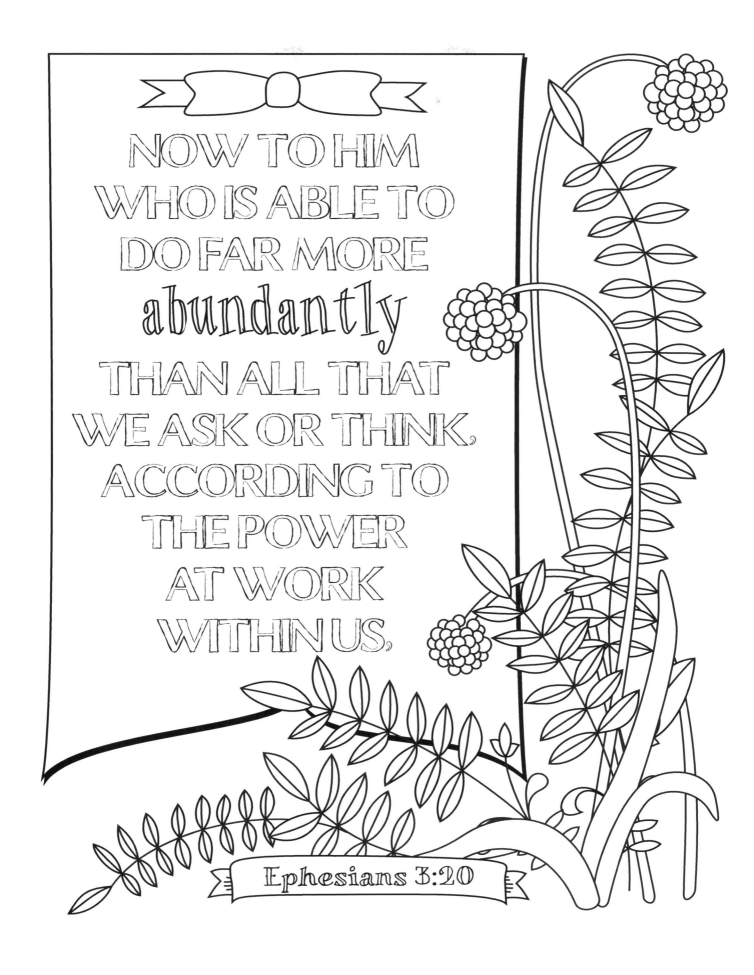

NOW TO HIM WHO IS ABLE TO DO FAR MORE abundantly THAN ALL THAT WE ASK OR THINK, ACCORDING TO THE POWER AT WORK WITHIN US,

Ephesians 3:20

Week 7

SCRIPTURE FOR THIS WEEK

2 Corinthians 12:7-10 ESV

[7] So to keep me from becoming conceited because of the surpassing greatness of the revelations, a thorn was given me in the flesh, a messenger of Satan to harass me, to keep me from becoming conceited. [8] Three times I pleaded with the Lord about this, that it should leave me. [9] But he said to me, "My grace is sufficient for you, for my power is made perfect in weakness." Therefore I will boast all the more gladly of my weaknesses, so that the power of Christ may rest upon me. [10] For the sake of Christ, then, I am content with weaknesses, insults, hardships, persecutions, and calamities. For when I am weak, then I am strong.

1 Samuel 1:1-20 ESV

There was a certain man of Ramathaim-zophim of the hill country of Ephraim whose name was Elkanah the son of Jeroham, son of Elihu, son of Tohu, son of Zuph, an Ephrathite. [2] He had two wives. The name of the one was Hannah, and the name of the other, Peninnah. And Peninnah had children, but Hannah had no children.

[3] Now this man used to go up year by year from his city to worship and to sacrifice to the Lord of hosts at Shiloh, where the two sons of Eli, Hophni and Phinehas, were priests of the Lord. [4] On the day when Elkanah sacrificed, he would give portions to Peninnah his wife and to all her sons and daughters. [5] But to Hannah he gave a double portion, because he loved her, though the Lord had closed her womb. [6] And her rival used to provoke her grievously to irritate her, because the Lord had closed her womb. [7] So it went on year by year. As often as she went up to the house of the Lord, she used to provoke her. Therefore Hannah wept and would not eat. [8] And Elkanah, her husband, said to her, "Hannah, why do you weep? And why do you not eat? And why is your heart sad? Am I not more to you than ten sons?"

[9] After they had eaten and drunk in Shiloh, Hannah rose. Now Eli the priest was sitting on the seat beside the doorpost of the temple of the Lord. [10] She was deeply distressed and prayed to the Lord and wept bitterly. [11] And she vowed a vow and said, "O Lord of hosts, if you will indeed look on the affliction of your servant and remember me and not forget your servant, but will give to your servant a son, then I will give him to the Lord all the days of his life, and no razor shall touch his head."

SCRIPTURE FOR THIS WEEK

[12] As she continued praying before the Lord, Eli observed her mouth. [13] Hannah was speaking in her heart; only her lips moved, and her voice was not heard. Therefore Eli took her to be a drunken woman. [14] And Eli said to her, "How long will you go on being drunk? Put your wine away from you." [15] But Hannah answered, "No, my lord, I am a woman troubled in spirit. I have drunk neither wine nor strong drink, but I have been pouring out my soul before the Lord. [16] Do not regard your servant as a worthless woman, for all along I have been speaking out of my great anxiety and vexation." [17] Then Eli answered, "Go in peace, and the God of Israel grant your petition that you have made to him." [18] And she said, "Let your servant find favor in your eyes." Then the woman went her way and ate, and her face was no longer sad.

[19] They rose early in the morning and worshiped before the Lord; then they went back to their house at Ramah. And Elkanah knew Hannah his wife, and the Lord remembered her. [20] And in due time Hannah conceived and bore a son, and she called his name Samuel, for she said, "I have asked for him from the Lord."

Psalm 37:7 ESV

[7] Be still before the Lord and wait patiently for him; fret not yourself over the one who prospers in his way, over the man who carries out evil devices!

Lamentations 3:25 ESV

[25] The Lord is good to those who wait for him, to the soul who seeks him.

SCRIPTURE FOR THIS WEEK

1 Kings 18:20-39 ESV

[20] So Ahab sent to all the people of Israel and gathered the prophets together at Mount Carmel. [21] And Elijah came near to all the people and said, "How long will you go limping between two different opinions? If the Lord is God, follow him; but if Baal, then follow him." And the people did not answer him a word. [22] Then Elijah said to the people, "I, even I only, am left a prophet of the Lord, but Baal's prophets are 450 men. [23] Let two bulls be given to us, and let them choose one bull for themselves and cut it in pieces and lay it on the wood, but put no fire to it. And I will prepare the other bull and lay it on the wood and put no fire to it. [24] And you call upon the name of your god, and I will call upon the name of the Lord, and the God who answers by fire, he is God." And all the people answered, "It is well spoken." [25] Then Elijah said to the prophets of Baal, "Choose for yourselves one bull and prepare it first, for you are many, and call upon the name of your god, but put no fire to it." [26] And they took the bull that was given them, and they prepared it and called upon the name of Baal from morning until noon, saying, "O Baal, answer us!" But there was no voice, and no one answered. And they limped around the altar that they had made. [27] And at noon Elijah mocked them, saying, "Cry aloud, for he is a god. Either he is musing, or he is relieving himself, or he is on a journey, or perhaps he is asleep and must be awakened." [28] And they cried aloud and cut themselves after their custom with swords and lances, until the blood gushed out upon them. [29] And as midday passed, they raved on until the time of the offering of the oblation, but there was no voice. No one answered; no one paid attention.

[30] Then Elijah said to all the people, "Come near to me." And all the people came near to him. And he repaired the altar of the Lord that had been thrown down. [31] Elijah took twelve stones, according to the number of the tribes of the sons of Jacob, to whom the word of the Lord came, saying, "Israel shall be your name," [32] and with the stones he built an altar in the name of the Lord. And he made a trench about the altar, as great as would contain two seahs of seed. [33] And he put the wood in order and cut the bull in pieces and laid it on the wood. And he said, "Fill four jars with water and pour it on the burnt offering and on the wood." [34] And he said,

SCRIPTURE FOR THIS WEEK

"Do it a second time." And they did it a second time. And he said, "Do it a third time." And they did it a third time. [35] And the water ran around the altar and filled the trench also with water.

[36] And at the time of the offering of the oblation, Elijah the prophet came near and said, "O Lord, God of Abraham, Isaac, and Israel, let it be known this day that you are God in Israel, and that I am your servant, and that I have done all these things at your word. [37] Answer me, O Lord, answer me, that this people may know that you, O Lord, are God, and that you have turned their hearts back." [38] Then the fire of the Lord fell and consumed the burnt offering and the wood and the stones and the dust, and licked up the water that was in the trench. [39] And when all the people saw it, they fell on their faces and said, "The Lord, he is God; the Lord, he is God."

John 1:16 ESV

[16] For from his fullness we have all received, grace upon grace.

Ephesians 3:20-21 ESV

[20] Now to him who is able to do far more abundantly than all that we ask or think, according to the power at work within us, [21] to him be glory in the church and in Christ Jesus throughout all generations, forever and ever. Amen.

Monday

READ: 2 Corinthians 12:7-10   **WRITE**: 2 Corinthians 12:8-9

1. Write out today's **SCRIPTURE** passage.

_____

_____

_____

_____

_____

_____

_____

_____

_____

_____

2. On the blank page to the right, **DRAW** or **WRITE** what this passage means to you.

3. My **PRAYER** for today:

_____

_____

_____

_____

_____

Monday

Tuesday

READ: 1 Samuel 1:1-20   **WRITE**: 1 Samuel 1:20

1. Write out today's **SCRIPTURE** passage.

_____

_____

_____

_____

_____

_____

_____

_____

_____

2. On the blank page to the right, **DRAW** or **WRITE** what this passage means to you.

3. My **PRAYER** for today:

_____

_____

_____

_____

LoveGodGreatly.com

Tuesday

Wednesday

READ: Psalm 37:7; Lamentations 3:25   **WRITE**: Psalm 37:7

1. Write out today's **SCRIPTURE** passage.

_____

_____

_____

_____

_____

_____

_____

_____

_____

_____

2. On the blank page to the right, **DRAW** or **WRITE** what this passage means to you.

3. My **PRAYER** for today:

_____

_____

_____

_____

_____

LoveGodGreatly.com

Wednesday

Thursday

READ: 1 Kings 18:20-39   **WRITE:** 1 Kings 18:38-39

1. Write out today's **SCRIPTURE** passage.

_____

_____

_____

_____

_____

_____

_____

_____

_____

2. On the blank page to the right, **DRAW** or **WRITE** what this passage means to you.

3. My **PRAYER** for today:

_____

_____

_____

_____

_____

Thursday

Friday

READ: John 1:16; Ephesians 3:20-21   **WRITE**: John 1:16; Ephesians 3:20

1. Write out today's **SCRIPTURE** passage.

_____

_____

_____

_____

_____

_____

_____

_____

_____

_____

2. On the blank page to the right, **DRAW** or **WRITE** what this passage means to you.

3. My **PRAYER** for today:

_____

_____

_____

_____

_____

Friday

This week I learned...

WEEK 7

Use the space below to draw a picture or write about what you learned this week from your time in God's Word.

Week 8

Prayer focus for this week: Spend time thanking God for how He is working in your life.

	Praying	Praise
Monday		
Tuesday		
Wednesday		
Thursday		
Friday		

Week 8

SCRIPTURE FOR THIS WEEK

Psalm 5:3 ESV

³ O Lord, in the morning you hear my voice; in the morning I prepare a sacrifice for you and watch.

Proverbs 8:17 ESV

¹⁷ I love those who love me, and those who seek me diligently find me.

Psalm 63:5-8 ESV

⁵ My soul will be satisfied as with fat and rich food, and my mouth will praise you with joyful lips, ⁶ when I remember you upon my bed, and meditate on you in the watches of the night; ⁷ for you have been my help, and in the shadow of your wings I will sing for joy. ⁸ My soul clings to you; your right hand upholds me.

Psalm 100 ESV

Make a joyful noise to the Lord, all the earth! ² Serve the Lord with gladness! Come into his presence with singing! ³ Know that the Lord, he is God! It is he who made us, and we are his; we are his people, and the sheep of his pasture. ⁴ Enter his gates with thanksgiving, and his courts with praise! Give thanks to him; bless his name! ⁵ For the Lord is good; his steadfast love endures forever, and his faithfulness to all generations.

Psalm 18:1-6 ESV

I love you, O Lord, my strength. ² The Lord is my rock and my fortress and my deliverer, my God, my rock, in whom I take refuge, my shield, and the horn of my salvation, my stronghold. ³ I call upon the Lord, who is worthy to be praised, and I am saved from my enemies.

SCRIPTURE FOR THIS WEEK

[4] The cords of death encompassed me; the torrents of destruction assailed me; [5] the cords of Sheol entangled me; the snares of death confronted me.

[6] In my distress I called upon the Lord; to my God I cried for help. From his temple he heard my voice, and my cry to him reached his ears.

Psalm 51 ESV

Have mercy on me, O God, according to your steadfast love; according to your abundant mercy blot out my transgressions. [2] Wash me thoroughly from my iniquity, and cleanse me from my sin!

[3] For I know my transgressions, and my sin is ever before me. [4] Against you, you only, have I sinned and done what is evil in your sight, so that you may be justified in your words and blameless in your judgment. [5] Behold, I was brought forth in iniquity, and in sin did my mother conceive me. [6] Behold, you delight in truth in the inward being, and you teach me wisdom in the secret heart.

[7] Purge me with hyssop, and I shall be clean; wash me, and I shall be whiter than snow. [8] Let me hear joy and gladness; let the bones that you have broken rejoice. [9] Hide your face from my sins, and blot out all my iniquities. [10] Create in me a clean heart, O God, and renew a right spirit within me. [11] Cast me not away from your presence, and take not your Holy Spirit from me. [12] Restore to me the joy of your salvation, and uphold me with a willing spirit.

[13] Then I will teach transgressors your ways, and sinners will return to you. [14] Deliver me from bloodguiltiness, O God, O God of my salvation, and my tongue will sing aloud of your righteousness. [15] O Lord, open my lips, and my mouth will declare your praise. [16] For you will not delight in sacrifice, or I would give it; you will not be pleased with a burnt offering. [17] The sacrifices of God are a broken spirit; a broken and contrite heart, O God, you will not despise.

[18] Do good to Zion in your good pleasure; build up the walls of Jerusalem; [19] then will you delight in right sacrifices, in burnt offerings and whole burnt offerings; then bulls will be offered on your altar.

Monday

READ: Psalm 5:3; Proverbs 8:17   **WRITE**: Psalm 5:3

1. Write out today's **SCRIPTURE** passage.

_____

_____

_____

_____

_____

_____

_____

_____

_____

_____

2. On the blank page to the right, **DRAW** or **WRITE** what this passage means to you.

3. My **PRAYER** for today:

_____

_____

_____

_____

_____

LoveGodGreatly.com

Monday

Tuesday

READ: Psalm 63:5-8   **WRITE**: Psalm 63:5-6

1. Write out today's **SCRIPTURE** passage.

_____

_____

_____

_____

_____

_____

_____

_____

_____

_____

2. On the blank page to the right, **DRAW** or **WRITE** what this passage means to you.

3. My **PRAYER** for today:

_____

_____

_____

_____

_____

Tuesday

Wednesday

READ: Psalm 100   **WRITE:** Psalm 100:4-5

1. Write out today's **SCRIPTURE** passage.

_____

_____

_____

_____

_____

_____

_____

_____

_____

_____

2. On the blank page to the right, **DRAW** or **WRITE** what this passage means to you.

3. My **PRAYER** for today:

_____

_____

_____

_____

_____

Wednesday

Thursday

1. Write out today's SCRIPTURE passage.

_____

_____

_____

_____

_____

_____

_____

_____

_____

2. On the blank page to the right, DRAW or WRITE what this passage means to you.

3. My PRAYER for today:

_____

_____

_____

_____

Thursday

Friday

READ: Psalm 51   **WRITE:** Psalm 51:2-4

1. Write out today's **SCRIPTURE** passage.

_____

_____

_____

_____

_____

_____

_____

_____

_____

2. On the blank page to the right, **DRAW** or **WRITE** what this passage means to you.

3. My **PRAYER** for today:

_____

_____

_____

_____

Friday

This week I learned...

WEEK 8

Use the space below to draw a picture or write about what you learned this week from your time in God's Word.

Let's create!

Color this bookmark and add your own designs and patterns to the back! When you're finished, cut out along the dotted lines and fold in half. Glue wrong sides together. Punch a hole in the top and add some ribbon. Keep it in your Bible or favorite book to remind you to love, do good, bless, and pray.

front

back

But I say to you who hear, love your enemies, do good to those who hate you, bless those who curse you, pray for those who abuse you.

Luke 6:27-28

Made in the USA
Lexington, KY
24 July 2016